STUPENDOUS SPORTS

CRACKING CRICKET

Robin Bennett

Robin is an author and entrepreneur who has written several books for children.

When Robin grew up he thought he wanted to be a cavalry officer until everyone else realised that putting him in charge of a tank was a very bad idea. He then became an assistant gravedigger in London. After that he had a career frantically starting businesses (everything from dog-sitting to sandwich making, tuition to translation)... until finally settling down to write improbable stories to keep his children from killing each other on long car journeys.

Robin plays most sports. Poorly.

Matt Cherry

Matt grew up on the Kent coast, writing and drawing, where he still lives today with his wife and two children. He still loves to write and draw every day, so he hasn't changed much really. He's just a lot taller.

CRACKING CRICKET

ROBIN BENNETT
ILLUSTRATED BY
MATT CHERRY

Firefly

First published in 2023
by Firefly Press
25 Gabalfa Road, Llandaff North,
Cardiff, CF14 2JJ
www.fireflypress.co.uk

Text © Robin Bennett 2023
Illustrations © Matt Cherry 2023
The author and illustrator assert their moral right to be
identified as author and illustrator in accordance with
the Copyright, Designs and Patent Act 1988.

A CIP catalogue record of this book
is available from the British Library.

ISBN 978-1-915444-21-9

*This book has been published with the support
of the Books Council of Wales.*

Design by: Tanwen Haf
Printed and bound by: CPI Group (UK) Ltd,
Croydon, Surrey CRO 4YY

FOREWORD

May I begin by saying cricket is such a wonderful sport. It's provided me with life experiences, friendships and memories that I will forever be grateful for.

I started my love for the game the same place that the majority of children do, in my parents' back garden. I recall long days spent with my two brothers with our imaginary test match scenarios: each pretending to be one of our heroes of the game. I was always Alan Donald trying to tear in from the bottom of the garden, through the flower beds and letting rip at whichever of my brothers was batting. They were the best days. I finished my career having played for eighteen years professionally, representing three counties and being part of an England side that won an Ashes series in 2005.

Cricket is a game which can be played by anyone; it's a game which I think produces critical thinking, concentration, discipline and courage. These are all values that can be transferred into the rest of life, so when I see men, women and children all playing and enjoying cricket, it does bring an enormous smile to my face!

To be asked to provide a brief foreword for this book was an offer I was delighted to accept. Promoting cricket in a positive, fun and educational way is hugely important for the game's development and for current and future generations of boys and girls. And this is something I will support with all the enthusiasm and energy I have.

Simon

SIMON JONES MBE,
GLAMORGAN, WORCESTERSHIRE.
HAMPSHIRE AND ENGLAND

CONTENTS

CHAPTER 1:
HISTORY OF THE GAME

What is cricket, who invented it and what's it got to do with killer robots?

Cricket is probably the most puzzling game ever invented.

Just read this old summary of the rules for the men's game if you don't believe me:

You have two sides: one out in the field and one in. Each man that's in the side that's in goes out, and when he's out he comes in and the next man goes in until he's out. When they are all out, the side that's out comes in and the side that's been in goes out and tries to get those coming in, out.

See?

To make matters worse, some people claim that it's not even a sport. Instead, they'll tell you (while putting on their serious face) that 'cricket is a way of life', or, even 'THE MEANING OF LIFE'.

So, it's either a bonkers *in when you're out, out when you're in* game or some kind of eccentric religion in which everyone plays outside and enjoys a good tea afterwards.

People can't even agree on how and when it started. The top five theories are that cricket was:

- Invented by people cheating at bowls.
- Played by kids in the south of England in the Middle Ages. (The Weald, to be precise, which is in Kent. How they know that, or why it should have been the Weald, no one seems keen to say.)
- Played by people in Flanders, or next door in France – and not just any old people: King Edward II was one of them apparently.
- Brought here by aliens – **Killer Robot Aliens**, to be precise.
- Made up by bored shepherds in England, anytime between about 1300 and 1600.

I'm going with the last one – those shepherds – because sheep can be hilarious and, as anyone who looks after them knows, when they're not trying to kill themselves sheep are pretty simple. They sort of look after themselves from sunrise to sunset, including all the eating and pooing in between.

This means that shepherds have a lot of time on their hands to invent a sport quite unlike any other and that, in itself, is quite funny.

But pinning it on shepherds makes sense, too. Early cricket balls would often

be made out of matted wool or from sheep's wool wrapped in leather; a shepherd carries a crook (stick) and players today stand in front of wickets (like a wicket gate that shepherds use when they are moving sheep around). As the ball was tossed to the batter, you can easily imagine someone shouting, 'Crook it!'

So, first prize for inventing cricket goes to bored shepherds with dozy sheep.

Anyway, whatever, after around the sixteenth century the history of cricket gets much clearer because people started to write about Cricket or 'Creckett'. A court case in 1550 mentions playing it at school, which is believed to be the first written reference to the game. Many believed it spent the next couple of hundred years being mainly played by kids (hurray!), until the adults decided it was far too much fun just to leave to kids and nicked it back (boo!).

By 1700 it had become the most popular sport in London among men and women ... and it started to spread.

In fact, after taking over London and the south of England, cricket got pretty adventurous and decided to miss out the north of England for the time being and try its luck in America and the Middle East. A game in Aleppo in Syria was written about in 1676! And the first-ever international match was played between the US and Canada in New York in 1844.

In spite of this, cricket never really caught on in Canada, presumably because Canada is often armour-plated in ice, and there doesn't seem to be any shortage of trees that bears might be hiding behind.

About this time (1800s), the bat was rapidly changing from what looked a bit like a hockey stick (or shepherd's crook – sorry to bang on about it) into something we might recognise today as a good, honest bat that knows its place. This was mainly because players had stopped rolling the ball along the ground in a nice safe way and were now trying to knock the wickets over (or the batter's head off) by bowling the ball overarm. Some comedian did come up with a bat that was as wide as the wicket, until everyone else put a stop to this and decided that the bat couldn't be wider than 4 inches (10.16 cm).

While we're on the subject of rules, no one can remember who thought up the basics, but a code of practice was drawn up by the Duke of Richmond and someone called Alan Brodick, in 1728. Probably quite useful (and a pretty typical thing for a duke and a mate or two to do) but they did have to wait another 40 odd years until the rules became proper rules that most people stuck to.

This probably goes a long way to explaining why, even today, cricket has real rules and rules that are more like guidelines – sort of *we prefer it that way and we'll be disappointed if you do it another way but there's not much we can do about it* rules.

This has led to cricket having a reputation for being just as much about fair play (the right way to play) than fixed laws (i.e., 'The Laws of Cricket') and it's certainly why a great many people on planet Earth think cricket is much better and more noble than other sports.

And they may be right because nowadays it's

the second largest sport in the world after football. It's true that the British Empire helped spread it in the first place, but it's long since been a much-loved sport around the world. In fact, it is enjoyed by more than 2.5 billion fans in 180 countries.

India and Pakistan are considered the biggest rivals in international cricket. And the rivalry is good for viewership, because it makes it more interesting. It is estimated that around 300 million people will tune in to watch nail-biting matches between these two nations.

COOL QUOTES

'I bowl so slowly that if I don't like a ball I can run after it and bring it back.'

– J.M. Barrie (creator of *Peter Pan*, so a great writer but a very poor cricketer, apparently).

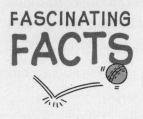

FASCINATING FACTS

Among Australian players and fans, the score considered unlucky is 87. They call it the Devil's number (in frightened whispers) because 87 taken away from 100 is 13.

A score of 111 in cricket is often called a Nelson. It's called that because of Admiral Nelson who'd spent a career fighting at sea busily losing bits of himself to cannon fire. At the end of his life, he had only 'One eye, one arm and one leg' (one, one, one or 111).

Note: This isn't true – Admiral Nelson still had both his legs when he died.

COOL QUOTES

Russell Crowe, New Zealand's famous Oscar-winning actor, who is a cousin of former Kiwi skippers Martin and Jeff Crowe, is a huge fan of the game, telling BBC cricket correspondent Jonathan Agnew on a visit to watch Australia play England in 2009 that it had

'been my dream for thirty years'

to go to the home of cricket – Lord's.

Great dates

○ **1550** First mention of cricket anywhere.

○ **1745** First recorded women's match.

○ **1751** First cricket match played in India (Calcutta Cricket Club).

○ **1772** First-class cricket begins, played at Broadhalfpenny Down, England, on 24 and 25 June.

○ **1787** Formation of Marylebone Cricket Club aka the MCC, at Lord's – perhaps the most famous cricket ground in the world and considered the home of cricket.

○ **1877** First Ashes match played to mark the first time England had lost to Australia on a world stage (in 1882). The Ashes trophy is a tiny urn that contains the ashes of the burned English bails.

○ **1900** Six-ball overs introduced (pretty important, take a look at the Appendix: 'Overs').

○ **1973** First World Cup took place, which was won by the host – the England's women's cricket team against Australia. The men's World Cup started two years later.

W.G. GRACE

No opening chapter on the splendid and fantastically strange game of cricket would be complete without talking in a bit of detail about the father of the modern game, Mr W.G. Grace.

First up, if you are going to be considered a giant in any game, not just cricket, it certainly helps if you are actually a giant and if you've got a beard that looks like an otter is clinging to your chin for dear life. Luckily for him, William Gilbert Grace was huge and had a very large beard indeed.

But he was also a superhumanly talented cricketer who almost single-handedly — through skill and colossal sportsmanship — created the game we know today.

Plus, he was a doctor.

But that's beside the point.

'They came to see me bat,
not you bowl.'

– W.G. Grace, putting the bails back on
his stumps after being bowled first ball.

W.G. Grace came from a family of cricketers, who loved winning the game as much as playing it. As a youth he'd been pretty good at other sports: as a hurdler at the National Olympian Games in 1866 and playing football for a London team, the Wanderers. By this time he had already started to play first-class cricket, at a time when the game was changing rapidly.

And no one else had a bigger hand in this change than W.G. Grace because it turned out he could bat, he could bowl, he could field and he was a brilliant tactician, all of which meant he captained most sides he played for. Other players said he hit the ball harder and straighter than anyone they had ever seen. And although he carried on bowling round arm (half way between underarm and overarm is the best way to describe it) when others were already bowling overarm, he still managed medium-fast pace and incredible accuracy. As a fielder, he could throw the ball like a trebuchet — once recording a 112-metre throw (the average adult can throw a ball a relatively pathetic 35 m). He explained this by saying he used to throw stones at crows a lot when he was growing up in the country.

In 1873 he became the first-ever player to score a thousand first-class runs in a season and get a hundred wickets. People were amazed. Then he proceeded to do the same thing every year until 1886.

And that really did it.

Very soon after, Grace became a superstar and people flocked to see him play, even in Australia. Although he could be a tough competitor and an argumentative player — as much over money as the rules — outside sport, he had a reputation for kindness. As a doctor, he very rarely charged anyone who was poor and he was greatly upset by World War One from a humanitarian point of view. Knowing when to be soft and when to be strict is the mark of any great cricketer, or sportsperson, for that matter. When he died in 1915, he was mourned by millions.

CHAPTER 2:
MEET THE PLAYERS

Let's play: Top Stumps!

There are eleven players per side in any cricket team that is playing a standard match against another side. All players need to be able to bat a bit, perhaps be able to bowl and certainly to field. But when and how often they do these things depends on how good they are at each skill ... and team tactics.

So any team will have their specialist bowlers (who don't bat much if they can help it), superstar batters (who nearly always can't bowl to save their miserable skins), at least one or two players who can catch better than trained seals and almost always one smart arse who can do everything, always gets picked first and probably has really cool hair.

BATTERS
THE OPENER

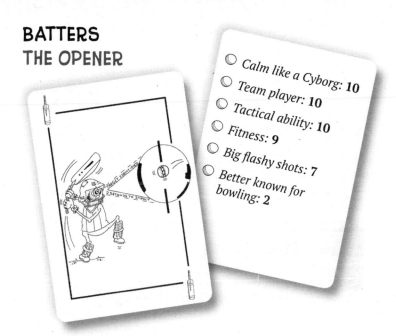

- Calm like a Cyborg: **10**
- Team player: **10**
- Tactical ability: **10**
- Fitness: **9**
- Big flashy shots: **7**
- Better known for bowling: **2**

Being an opener is a bit like being the eldest child in the family: no one expects too much of you, because you've come along first, so they don't have any strong opinions yet, but they've still got pretty high hopes either way. You can do nothing wrong, so it's not going to be all your fault if the match is lost but, then again, you're not likely to do anything completely right according to a lot of people who think they are experts. So as you both walk out onto the pitch, people will be telling you to, 'just stay in, whatever' and others will be hoping you get out quickly so they can have a go at batting. At the same time, you can't just hang about, prodding at the odd ball or two until it starts to get dark.

People want runs! But not too fast, or you might get yourself out, and the next batter hasn't finished their cake ... and their tea is still too hot to drink.

A successful opener needs to listen with half an ear to his or her captain but also needs to feel the rhythm of the game – and the scoring pace they need to set.

They are cricket Jedi.

THE TOP ORDER

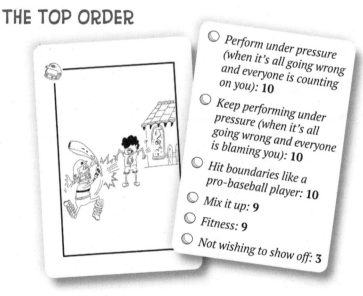

- Perform under pressure (when it's all going wrong and everyone is counting on you): **10**
- Keep performing under pressure (when it's all going wrong and everyone is blaming you): **10**
- Hit boundaries like a pro-baseball player: **10**
- Mix it up: **9**
- Fitness: **9**
- Not wishing to show off: **3**

You know you are one of two or three of the best batters on the side, let's get that out of the way right now and this is almost certainly why you're in the team. This is great but people also expect a lot of you. How you feel, as you make your way out onto the pitch, depends on how well the openers have done. If they've scored a bunch of runs, you'll probably be thinking of adding a bunch more quite quickly (and worried that you might not). If they both got out first ball, then everyone is looking to you to turn things around. You have to be able to score quickly, but you need almost the same amount of patience as an opener. When all is said and done, you are the best chance the side has to win the game.

Does that scare you? Possibly ... then again, possibly not because, as I say, you know you're good.

THE MIDDLE ORDER

- Calm like a Cyborg: **10**
- Hang on in there: **10**
- Save the day: **10**
- Big flashy shots: **10**
- Cunning: **9**
- Fitness: **9**
- Better known for bowling or fielding: **6**

The middle-order batter is often the person people most want to be friends with, because you're basically an opener who doesn't take him or herself too seriously. You probably suspect you can bat better or at least as well as the top order (if you could be bothered) but you are far too busy saving the day by going out there smashing boundaries or smiling sadly to yourself when you get out first ball and shrugging as if you don't care. But that is not true, you care a lot, and you know that you are the last line of defence, the last batter who has a decent chance of turning things around. You could have been a hero.

And you are, often enough, to make this a great role in the team.

THE LOWER ORDER

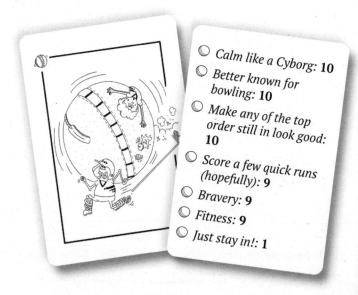

○ Calm like a Cyborg: **10**
○ Better known for bowling: **10**
○ Make any of the top order still in look good: **10**
○ Score a few quick runs (hopefully): **9**
○ Bravery: **9**
○ Fitness: **9**
○ Just stay in!: **1**

If this innings was a concert, you're the guy who comes on right at the end to play the national anthem on the triangle, just when everyone is preparing to leave. You're a bowler, for crying out loud, and now another bowler is trying to knock your head off so they can wrap things up and get into a nice hot shower.

The best you can hope is that there is a really good batter at the other end, and it's your job to stay in, so they can score a few more runs. But most people think that's unlikely to happen: you're the tail ender, it's almost all over...

...or is it?

There've been enough big scores by lower-order batters since the invention of cricket, enough turnarounds thanks to these so-called 'no hopers' for there always to be a faint glimmer, a razor-slim chance, a distant light wavering in the darkness of the eternal teatime.

And today is that day.

Finally you get to feel what it is like to be a proper batter for one brief but marvellous moment of glory.

As you score the winning run, a beam of light breaks through the cloud and you stand tall in your pads, raising a bat – like the sword of Gryffindor – and hear the roar of the crowds shouting your name, like the great heroes of old: 'Darren, Darren, Darren.'

But, then again, it's unlikely.

BOWLERS

THE FAST OR 'PACE' BOWLER

- Bowl – like – really, really fast: **10**
- Fear factor: **10**
- Fitness: **9**
- Tactics: **8**
- Modesty: **6**
- Batting: **2**

At Stupendous Sports HQ, we think that every bowler when they start out wants to be a fast bowler. I mean, bowling really fast kind of makes sense if you want to get as many batters out as possible (as long as you're on target). Plus it's great fun.

But, like all bowlers, a fast bowler needs a plan, so being good at tactics is essential. There might be thirteen players out there on the pitch but it's a private war between you and the batter each time you run up to bowl. And so you need to be able to vary your bowling, depending on whether you want to hit the stumps or trick the batter into giving a catch.

So you need to be aggressive but super sneaky: a mixture between Thor and Loki.

And it's essential you are as fit as can be, as fast bowling means long run-ups: on average, they reckon a fast bowler will do more running than any other player – up to and over 4 miles a match (that's 6.5 km).

THE MEDIUM PACE BOWLER

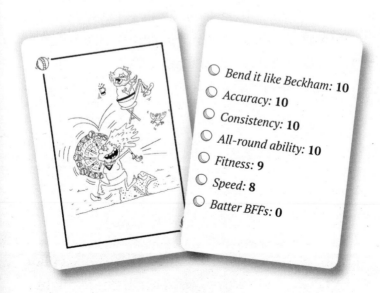

Bend it like Beckham: **10**
Accuracy: **10**
Consistency: **10**
All-round ability: **10**
Fitness: **9**
Speed: **8**
Batter BFFs: **0**

Where a professional fast bowler will be able to reach speeds of around 145 kilometres an hour (see page 68), a medium pace bowler will not be quite that speedy – around 113 km per hour. That's still as quick as a car in the fast lane on a motorway, mind. But what they lack in killer pace, they make up for in being able to use the shape of the ball to make life miserable for a batter.

This usually means making the ball swing (curve) through the air or bounce oddly off the seam (stitching) of the ball.

A medium pace bowler needs to combine the fitness and speed of a fast bowler and the clever hands and fingers of the spin bowler. You might not be as flashy as the pace bowlers or spinners but no one is ever going to say you don't get results and anyone who knows anything about cricket will be glad to have you on their team.

You are often the team all-rounder (see page 35).

THE SPIN BOWLER

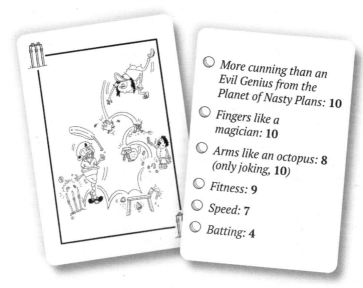

○ *More cunning than an Evil Genius from the Planet of Nasty Plans:* **10**

○ *Fingers like a magician:* **10**

○ *Arms like an octopus:* **8** *(only joking,* **10***)*

○ *Fitness:* **9**

○ *Speed:* **7**

○ *Batting:* **4**

Spin bowling is 'art meets sport'. Some of the greatest moments in cricket, if not the greatest moments in sport, have happened when a spin bowler is working their magic.

A spin bowler is unique because of the amount of practice and bravery they need. Because, on the day, the ball might not spin, or not spin very much or not in the way you want it to and that's got nothing to do with you (it's often the state of the ball, the pitch or the weather).

We've put down 9 for fitness because it's good to be fit for playing any kind of sport but a spin bowler is the one spot you can claim on the team if you're not that fast or athletic. People may look at you and wonder why you're on the side ... until you bowl a ball that dips in the air when you release it, then bounces off the pitch like a spider jumping sideways.

THE FIELDER

Catching a ball: **10**
Running after a ball: **10**
Diving on a ball: **10**
Stopping a ball: **10**
Concentration: **10**
Bravery: **10**
Patience: **10**

Everyone has to field in cricket – there's no getting out of it – and so everyone has to get good at it. One of the hardest things is spending what seems like days standing miles away from the action, to have your daydreaming broken by shouts of, 'Catch it, you dozy idiot!' And that's just from your mum.

So, in spite of what it looks like, you're not going to be able to use the spare time making daisy chains or catching up on chat groups. The best fielders are dedicated to the team and to working to get better.

We're all fielders: it just depends what type of one you want to be.

THE WICKET KEEPER

○ Catching the ball: **100**

○ Squatting for hours: **10**

○ Then leaping sideways at very short notice: **10**

○ Focus: **10**

○ Ability to pick up small things in big gloves: **8**

○ Run for the bus (with pads on): **3**

You need to have the concentration of a dog watching a clumsy toddler eating a cheeseburger: something is bound to happen and you need to be the first to react, it just depends when. Apart from the umpires, you are probably the only person who has to follow every ball while your side is fielding, except you'll be wearing great big things strapped to your legs, called 'pads', a hat (or helmet) and gloves, regardless of how hot it gets. This is not a role for dreamers or people who get fascinated by clouds or enjoy small talk.

You are the cricket version of a goalkeeper: rock solid and dependable, with the reactions of a Ninja.

GREAT STATS!

England wicket keeper Jonny Bairstow is an example to younger players of how the game is changing and an example to wicket keepers the world over. A huge scorer of quick, aggressive runs that can change a game in a few overs. Here's some stats: Jonny is the only English wicket keeper to get nine players out in a Test match – twice! As a wicket keeper he has got the most people out in a year (70 in 2016). And he has scored the highest number of Test runs as a wicket keeper in a year (1,470 in 2016). Pretty impressive.

OTHER PLAYERS YOU SHOULD KNOW ABOUT
THE ALL-ROUNDER

You know that the top order wish they could bowl like you and the opening bowlers wish they could bat like you. Secretly you think you should be team captain – but you often are, so that's OK then. If people think you might be a bit too much of a clever clogs, they don't mind because they know

you can save the match. Also, all-rounders tend to be the ones who don't take the game as seriously as everyone else. Probably because they are good enough not to need to and it explains why they usually look like they're having a great time.

COOL QUOTES

'That's the great thing about being an all-rounder. You can impose yourself on the game with bat and ball.'

– Ben Stokes, England men's captain

THE NIGHTWATCHMAN

This role doesn't exist in any other sport because not many other sports have matches that go on for days – unless you are talking golf, or football in the thirteenth century.

The Nightwatchman is someone who is not much good at batting, who comes on near the end of the day in a test match. The idea is that you don't want to lose one of your best players right at the end of the day. That said, the Nightwatchman has to stay in, so they can't be that bad. So you have to be the best of the bad players: one who can play defensively in the evening, then come along the next day and score lots of runs, hopefully quite quickly. There's been quite a few centuries (100 runs) scored by Nightwatchmen. Mark Boucher of South Africa is considered to have been one of the best. But spare a thought for poor old Alex Tudor of England, who scored 99 runs, not out: winning the match for his team but also ending it just before he got to the magic 100.

**'I can't really say I'm batting badly.
I'm not batting long enough
to be batting badly.'**

– Greg Chappell, former Australian cricketer

A FUNNY THING HAPPENED...

Shahid Afridi was asked to play a One
Day International (ODI) against Sri
Lanka in 1996 but he forgot his bat.
Borrowing one from Sachin Tendulkar,
Afridi scored what was then the fastest
century in ODI history – in 37 balls
(including 11 sixes and 6 fours).
Even Tendulkar's bat could
do great things!

FASCINATING FACTS

Cricket superstitions: the player with the weirdest rituals before playing was possibly Neil McKenzie of South Africa. While waiting to go out, he would tape his cricket bat to the ceiling. Before starting his innings, he would also check all the changing room lights to make sure they were off and check that the toilet seats were down.

Slightly fascinating note on fascinating fact: McKenzie started sticking his bat to the ceiling after his teammates did it as a joke.

New Zealander Amelia Kerr is the youngest cricketer to ever score 200 runs or more (aka a 'double century'). Aged just 17, she scored 232 runs against Ireland in 2018.

SACHIN TENDULKAR

Considered by many to be the finest batsman to have played the game in the modern era, and with very good reason.

Sachin (nicknamed the Little Master — as he is quite short at 165 cm played his first test match for India at the age of just 16 in 1989.

Tendulkar was the first-ever batsman in the history of cricket to score 12,000 test runs, then 13,000, then 14,000. He eventually retired with just under 16,000 test cricket runs, far higher than any other batter — a record that is unlikely to be beaten for a very long time. He's also the only batter to have scored 100 centuries in international cricket.

In 2013 he was chosen to be in the all-time Test Cricket World XI. Only one other modern cricketer — Viv Richards — made this fantasy team. Tendulkar holds the Khel Ratna Award, the highest Indian sporting award; and the Bharat Ratna Award, the highest Indian civilian honour, among loads of other awards.

So what was his secret?

True, he was quite aggressive, making use of a very original 'punch style' of cricket and added some pretty unusual shots to his armoury as he got older and was less bendy.

However, everyone seems to agree it was Tendulkar's perfect balance and calmness that set him apart from many other cricketers. Rock solid – never any waving the bat about unnecessarily, he played a classical style of cricket that was as stylish as it was simple.

Tendulkar is proof that if you get the basics right, greatness will follow.

Oh, and he could bowl pretty well, too.

CHAPTER 3:
THE MATCH

*In when you're out, out when you're in
and other mysteries explained*

THE PITCH

A cricket ground generally has to have two things
– otherwise it's just a medium-sized field and
should really have sheep in it:

1. There's the pitch – the hopefully nice and flat
   bit in the middle-ish where the batters stand
   and the bowlers bowl. It's sometimes called the
   'square', which, if we're being pedantic, is a fib
   because it's actually a rectangle, unless there
   are a few, side by side, which there often are.
2. Then there's the rest of the ground, which is
   also hopefully in a pretty good state with a
   boundary: this is the edge of the playing area,
   and it shouldn't be too far away, but also not
   too boringly easy to reach if you give the ball a
   good hard whack (with a decent bat).

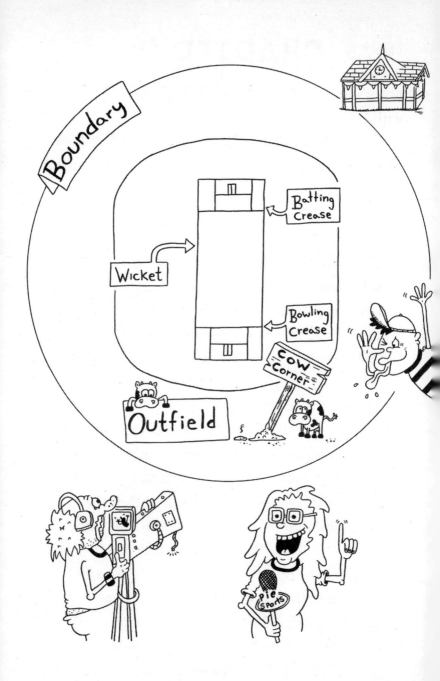

I say hopefully, as quite a lot of cricket-ground planners (mainly in schools and villages up and down the country) think it's funny to mess about with this perfectly reasonable model.

Here at Stupendous Sports HQ, we have seen it all. For example:

- A pitch perched on top of a steep hill. This meant that once the ball travelled further than a few yards, it sped up and rolled into the next county. On the other hand, the view was lovely.
- A pitch where mid-wicket is a large tree. There was something strange about this tree: once you noticed it (very hard not to), it was virtually impossible to hit the ball anywhere else.
- An outfield which had had cows in it until that morning, leaving almost no time for the cowpats to dry. Once the ball landed in a cowpat, it behaved very oddly and was also quite smelly.

So, it turns out that as long as the pitch is big enough and about the right shape, people will turn up and play.

Interesting note: There's actually a fielding position called Cow Corner. It's somewhere around deep mid-wicket (see page 56) and it's called that because it was usually a corner of the field in which it was safe for cows to happily munch and poo because very few batters hit the ball in that direction.

EQUIPMENT

So what does today's cricketer need?

That depends on whether they are fielding, wicket keeping, bowling, batting ... or umpiring.

Fielder

◯ Remember to wear trousers (advisable, but not essential)

◯ Shoes you can run after balls in (with bobbles or spikes on the soles)

◯ Sun cream (if hot) or jumper (if cold) or both (if playing in Britain)

◯ Hat.

Wicket keeper

○ Big gloves that – to start with – actually seem to make it harder to catch the ball. However, they stop your hands hurting and, once you get used to them, they're your best friends.

○ Helmet

○ Pads

○ Box.

Batter

- ◯ Small gloves, with protection on knuckles
- ◯ Helmet, to protect important brain
- ◯ Pads
- ◯ Box
- ◯ Chest guard
- ◯ Thigh pads
- ◯ Shoes – spikes and toe protection.

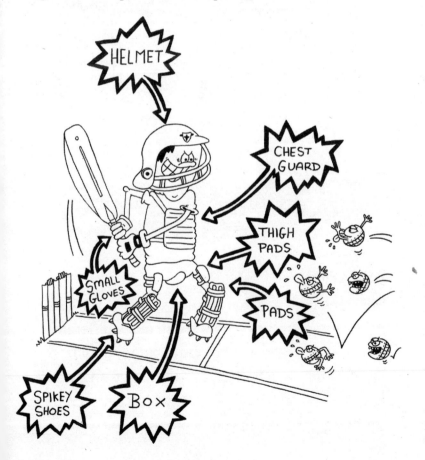

Umpire

- ⚪ White coat
- ⚪ Floppy hat
- ⚪ Over counter (or small stones)
- ⚪ Ten jumpers, all belonging to players.

DURATION

How long does a match last exactly? This is where it gets interesting. As there are so many different formats to cricket, and because a game should usually end when both sides have batted and are all out, cricket matches can last anything between the time it takes to brush your teeth to ... pretty much forever.

FASCINATING FACT

The longest Test match ever to have been played was between England and South Africa – it went on for nearly two weeks! The Timeless Test of 1939 started on Friday 3 March and it ended an exhausting 12 days later. There were a whopping 1,981 runs scored and 5,447 balls bowled. And, after all that, it was eventually declared a draw – if they'd carried on the England team would have missed their boat home!

To keep things simple, if we ignore – just for the time being – cricket played in your back garden, indoors (school corridors are great but probably not allowed) or the new 'The Hundred', there are currently three main formats in the international game:

- **Test Matches**
  5 days (usually) with two innings a side
- **One Day Internationals (aka ODIs)**
  Er, 1 day (or a bit less, if everyone is out quickly)
- **Twenty20 Internationals (aka T20s)**
  20 overs per side = 6 balls per over, or 120 chances to hit the ball very hard for each team. It's usually finished in three or four hours.

All formats can be very exciting for different reasons: Twenty20 because it's like a sprint to get runs – a stupendous slog; ODIs because there's still a lot that can go right or very wrong in one day and there's nearly always something happening. And Test matches because there's no game format quite like it in any sport, anywhere in the world. To people who don't understand cricket, Test matches can look like nothing is going on for hours – and sometimes it seems they are right: the bowlers bowl, batters push the ball about, the sun shines, birds sing high in a pale blue sky ... and you begin to doze off. THEN! TOTALLY without warning, the ball is in the air, the bowler shouts and a fielder (who was dozing off, too) wakes up, squints into the air, looking for a small red dot and dives...

Test Match cricket is like a game of chess but chess with great feats of physical bravery and acrobatic skill somehow added.

At Stupendous Sports HQ, we've seen five-day games lost in the space of an hour or fought to the last minute of the last day.

Test Cricket, at its best, is better than the best of anything else you might play or watch. Fact.

SCORING

To score in cricket you need to get runs, and to get those you need to run. It's really that simple. The trick (for the batter) is to hit the ball where there are no fielders, or as far away from them as possible. If he or she can do this, then there's time to run from one set of stumps, or wickets, to the other before the fielders get the ball back – this gets you one whole run.

The other batter has to run between the wickets too, so when you cross over try not to run into each other.

If you manage to hit the ball really far from any fielders, who then have to scamper about to go and get it, you'll have plenty of time to both run back again, to the end where you started (this gets you two runs), or three if both you and the other batter are one of the 0.01% of the population who have learned to run fast while wearing pads and possibly a box, in a helmet.

However, it gets better, because if you whack the ball all the way to the boundary (see page 42) you get four runs, or a whopping six runs if the ball goes over the boundary without bouncing first.

'I'm obsessed with cricket.'

– Daniel Radcliffe (part-time
wizard and cricket boffin)

GETTING OUT

At times it seems there are more disasters lurking that can lead to being 'out' in cricket than there are ways to stay in. This has something to do with the fact that, while you're batting, you are completely outnumbered: just two of you against eleven people all trying to make bad things happen to you. So it's a pretty unfriendly place out there.

When we say disasters, what we really mean is one of several unfortunate events that end up with you walking off the field, shaking your head as if life is very unfair.

(It's not, cricket is about the fairest sport in the known universe).

To keep things simple, there are only actually two ways that you can get out in cricket:

○ Being caught
○ Losing your wicket.

1. Caught

To be caught out, the bowler bowls a ball at you – without breaking any rules like bowling too close when you're not ready or bowling miles off target ('wide') – and you hit it, either with your bat or your gloves. And then a fielder catches it, before it bounces.

Nowadays, they have special machines with amazing hearing, like electronic rabbits, (that can detect whether you have hit the ball even if it has hardly touched your bat or glove at all.

2. Losing your wicket

You can lose your wicket in the following ways:

 If the bowler bowls and hits your stumps so that the bails fall off, then you're out.

 If the ball would have hit your stumps but your legs rather than the bat got in the way, you are also out. It's called Leg Before Wicket (LBW) and has been the second largest cause of arguments about sport in your front room and on the telly in sport history (right after the offside rule in football).

 If a fielder hits your stumps holding the ball, or by throwing it at the wicket and knocking the bails off, and you are out of your crease (see page 42), then, yup, you're also out. Sorry.

FIELDING POSITIONS

Each part of the pitch where a fielder can stand has a name. Some names are more ridiculous than others.

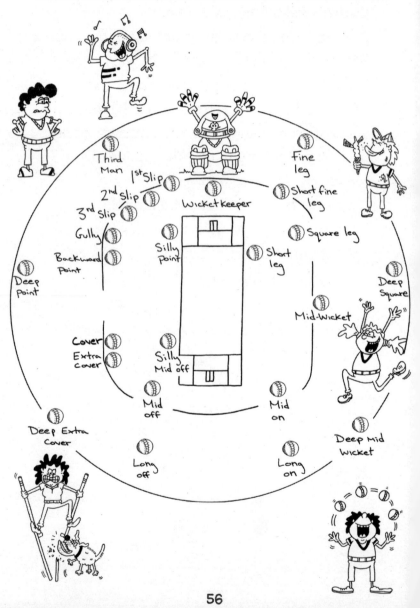

RULES

One of the interesting things about cricket is the difference between:

- Things you probably shouldn't do
- Things you definitely shouldn't do.

For example, it's not against the rules of cricket to bowl what people sometimes call a 'bouncer'. This is a ball that is bowled fast and hard into the ground ('short') so it bounces up and can hit the batter. It's quite scary. Nevertheless, bowlers are still allowed to bowl short and hard, but if you bowl too many of them, or if the umpire thinks the batter is too inexperienced or not good enough to cope, the umpire will put a stop to it pretty quick.

The Marylebone Cricket Club lists 42 types of unfair behaviour, where it is up to the players, led by the team captains, to be good sports and do what is right in the spirit of the game. Or it is up to the umpire to use their common sense and sense of fair play to have a gentle word with the players and politely ask them to stop doing whatever it is.

It's interesting that cricket umpires don't need to carry whistles.

So that just leaves us with the things you definitely shouldn't do. These fit into the following categories:

Batting
- You must not hit the ball twice on purpose
- You must not touch the ball with your hands
- You must not stop a fielder from getting to the ball ('obstruction').

Fielding

◯ You must not stop the batter from running between the wickets (also 'obstruction')

◯ You must not put the batter off (for example, by shouting 'watch out' for no reason, playing bagpipes badly, or pretending to be an aeroplane in the outfield).

Bowling

◯ You must not bowl the ball too far away from the batter ('wide').

◯ You must not bowl the ball with your foot over the crease (see page 42) ('no ball').

◯ You must not throw the ball (bending elbow too much).

Everyone

◯ Do what the umpire says. End of story.

CRACKING CRICKET GROUNDS

Galle, Sri Lanka
Capacity 35,000
Built 1876
Why do we like it?
In spite of being almost completely destroyed in the 2004 tsunami, Galle is one of the nicest grounds there is. Party atmosphere for the big matches.

Malahide, Dublin, Ireland
Capacity 11,000
Built 1861
Why do we like it?
Home of Irish cricket and venue for Ireland's first test match against Pakistan in 2018.

Newlands, Cape Town, South Africa
Capacity 17,000
Built 1889
Why do we like it?
It's got a giant mountain next door. Stunning.

Trent Bridge, Nottingham, England
Capacity 17,000
Built 1841
Why do we like it?
Although it doesn't have the history of the Oval or Lord's in London, a lot of people still think it is the most amazing traditional cricket venue in the world. History has been made here more times than you can count. Best-looking scoreboard in the world.

MCG, Melbourne, Australia
Capacity 96,000!
Built 1854
Why do we like it?
The noisiest cricket you will ever watch.

Feroz Shah Kotla, India
Capacity 40,000
Built 1883
Why do we like it?
Huge atmosphere, hardest place to play away in the world.

***Queens Park Oval, Port of Spain,
Trinidad and Tobago***
Capacity 25,000
Built 1896
Why do we like it?
Caribbean carnival cricket at its best.

Lord's, London, England
Capacity 28,000
Built 1814
Why do we like it?
Home of cricket.
Say no more.

CHAPTER 4:
SKILLS AND TACTICS

Including useful tricks to amaze your friends and crush your enemies

Cricket may look hard to play but it's actually one of the easiest sports to get involved with: if you're not much good at batting, then the chances are you might be able to bowl a bit; if your bowling makes everyone point and laugh, then fielding might be your thing – even if that just means getting in the way of the ball by falling over; and if none of those work out for you, then learning the rules and understanding the game inside out can turn you into the cunning tactician (captain!) every great team needs. So, you've got quadruple the chance over most other sports of finding a place in any side and feeling like a valued member of the team.

You don't even have to be an especially fast runner, a good jumper, strong, tall etc. Good cricketers come in all shapes and sizes: it's the ultimate team sport in that respect.

However, like all sports, you should start by trying everything, and know that practising the core skills makes all the difference. To help you on your path to cricketing superstardom, here's the Stupendous Sports Cricket Skills and Tactics chapter.

If you're going to read anything before walking onto a pitch, this should be it.

BOWLING

Basics

If the object of the game is to get as many batters out as quickly as possible, it's obvious that being accurate in bowling is going to be important. This means bowling the ball where you want it to go, and not just chucking it vaguely in the direction of the batter and hoping it doesn't hit a passing bird or go backwards and break someone's window.

Most of the time, this means bowling at the three stumps but, in a game where catches or being caught LBW can get a batter out, being able to bowl different types of ball is a definite advantage. Mix it up, basically.

To master bowling you need to work on the following three basics:

1. Run-up

This is the engine of bowling: it powers speed and accuracy. Find a run-up you are comfortable with for the type of bowling you do: try a few things out. Fast bowlers usually have a long run-up of around 15–20 paces, medium pacers slightly less and spin bowlers around six paces – when it's more of a gentle stroll you might take with a very elderly relative than bounding towards the crease like a furious cow.

2. Arm swing

Bowling is very different from throwing – the arm is straighter and should swing past your ear (a bit like a windmill sail going round). Watch videos online and work out a way of doing it that doesn't take too much effort – being loose and relaxed is ideal. Working on your flexibility helps a lot.

3. Release

It sounds obvious but we're going to say it anyway: don't let go of the ball until you are ready. If you release the ball a fraction too early it'll probably go too high and risk knocking the batter's head off (and you won't be popular); release too late and it'll bang into the ground, trickle down the wicket and come to a stop about a metre in front of the batter.

If this sounds hard, then it might make you feel better to know that most of the time your brain will tell you when to release the ball, without you having to think too much. In fact, thinking too hard about the release is not a great idea.

Just relax, have fun, and the basics will fall into place with time and a bit of practice.

Not the basics

Right, so you've taken our advice, worked at the basics and you're no longer a danger to yourself and others, so it's time to develop into the type of bowler you want to be.

NOTE *If your foot goes over the crease (see page 42) it's a 'no ball' so the batter is not out even if you hit the stumps, and the other team gets one free run (or two in some forms of the game – like T20 or ODIs) and you have to bowl an extra ball.*

GREAT STATS Shoaib Akhtar, aka the 'Rawalpindi Express', is the quickest bowler the world has ever seen. The pacer from Pakistan bowled the fastest delivery in international cricket during the Cricket World Cup in 2003. It hurtled down the wicket at 161.3 km per hour

FAST BOWLING

This is (obviously) when you try and bowl as fast as you can while staying accurate. To get as fast as possible, you need run-up speed, arm-swing speed and body strength.

○ Practise running up and placing your front foot on the same spot of the crease each time as you swing your arm around. Use your whole body (not just arms and legs) to make the ball go faster. It's not a bad idea to get a mate to film you doing this and see how you look. Like a lot of things in sport, if you look good doing it, then you probably are good.

○ Concentrate on swinging your arm the same way each time (be careful not to bend the elbow, which is throwing) and work on 'snapping' your wrist straight at the last moment.

○ Practise holding the ball in different ways, as this makes the ball fly through the air and bounce differently.

For example:

Seam bowlers hold the ball with two fingers along the seam (stitching of the ball), so it lands on the stitching and bounces left or right, which is nearly always a nasty surprise for the batter.

Swing bowlers do roughly the same, but they shine one side of the ball on their trousers, and this makes the ball curve in the air. It's sort of like a magic trick and it's very hard to hit a curving ball (or a curving anything for that matter).

○ Finally, go running and go to the gym – fast bowling is a good excuse to get fast, fit and strong.

SPIN BOWLING

Important note: the following instructions are for people who are right handed. If you're left handed, everything is the other way around. As usual.

If you find that speed is making you inaccurate or you just don't fancy starting your run-ups in the car park, spin bowling might be for you. There are two basic types of spin bowler: the off spinner and the leg spinner.

Off spinner (bowling 'off breaks')

This is one of the most common types of spin
bowling. Hold the ball along the ridge of the
stitching and, as you release the ball, flick down
and to the right with your wrist, index finger and
middle finger. The harder you flick, the more the
ball will spin and so the further it will jump from
the outside off stump where you usually want it to
land and fly confusingly towards the middle or leg
stump and fool the batter.

Spin grip

Leg spinner ('leg break')

The ball will bounce the other way with leg spin (from right to left: pitching near the leg stump and spinning towards the off side). Roll the wrist the other way, anti-clockwise – a bit like you're twisting a door knob to the left, and flick your fingers left. Your middle finger will do most of the work.

This takes practice but good leg spinners are rare and nearly always get picked.

So there you go. As I said, it's a good idea to watch as many videos of people doing it as you can – seeing is as much help as doing when it comes to bowling.

USEFUL TRICKS

The Yorker

This is a useful ball for getting people out. There's no seam, spin or swing quite often, you just bowl it 'long' so it bounces very close to the batter's feet, goes under the bat and hits the wicket. It's a very good fast ball to learn early on.

The Googly

Basically, it looks like a leg break, but you twist your hand right around, so it is actually an off break. From where the batter is standing, he or she will expect it to spin from left to right, instead it bounces right to left.

The Flipper

Hold the ball for a leg spin but instead of rolling your wrist or flicking your fingers, 'snap' the ball instead, like you are trying to snap your fingers – pinching the ball between your fingers and thumb. A good Flipper will be faster than a normal leg break. It won't spin and will hardly bounce.

The slower ball

Nice one to start with. Bowl several balls at full speed, huffing and puffing away. Then, looking very angry with the batter, take a good long, fast run-up, giving the impression you're planning on putting everything into this ball.

Then bowl a slower ball than you've done so far, but right on stump.

With any luck, the batter will be so convinced your ball is going to come at them like a meteorite entering the Earth's atmosphere, they'll take a wild swing at it, but far too early, miss by a mile ... and your ball will knock the bails off.

BATTING

Seeing as the aim of batting is to hit the ball as far as you can, and in the direction you want it to go, the main skill is getting a wide-ish stick to connect with a ball the size of an orange that is going very fast or doing all sorts of strange things. Or both.

Here's where you've got a couple of million years of hunter-gatherer instincts on your side when it comes to hitting things with what is essentially a wooden club: and whether it's the top of a mammoth's head, someone called Ug you don't get on with, or a small red leathery ball is neither here nor there.

That said, there are a few things you can do to make you better at it and it's worth getting right because there's nothing better than the feeling of hitting a ball out of the ground for six runs.

76

Stupendous Sports Ultimate Guide to Batting

◯ Stand side-on to the bowler, feet apart (roughly the same width as your shoulders).

◯ Hold the bat in both hands, close together, so it feels comfortable (ask someone to show you exactly how, if you like).

◯ Make sure your bat is in line with the stumps – usually the middle one (ask the umpire, if you are unsure).

◯ Tap the bat on the ground – if only to show the bowler you are ready, but it also looks like you mean business.

◯ Bring the bat back and hold it off the ground between 30 and 60 cm up (to give you your swing).

◯ As the ball comes down the wicket, watch it very carefully.

◯ As the ball bounces, you can move the bat in a downward swing.

◯ Aim to hit or block the ball (see 'Strokes').

◯ Follow through with your swing (important – even if you miss – it's a very good habit to get into).

Useful tricks

◯ Start by hitting something soft, like a tennis ball, then a rubber practice ball before moving on to the real thing.

○ Concentrate on your breathing – it helps you to stay calm and hit the ball well.

○ Move your feet, stepping forward, with your front foot roughly in line with where the ball bounces is a good way of never missing it.

Different strokes

Different strokes will affect the direction the ball will go:

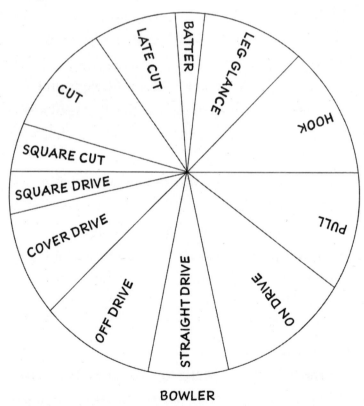

BOWLER

Here are some different strokes to work on, depending on where the ball lands and how it bounces.

Forward and back defensive:
Absolutely the first thing you need to get the hang of. If you can do this, you'll almost never get out. Depending on where the ball lands (long, with the ball bouncing close to the batter's feet or short, bouncing further up the wicket, away from the batter), step forward or step back and block the ball. Nothing fancy but effective at stopping the ball from hitting the wicket. However, you won't score many runs this way.

Drive
Learning to drive a straight-ish ball (one that's coming right at you) will score runs. It's basically a forward defensive but you hit the ball harder and follow through more, so the ball runs along the ground, very fast, left or right of the bowler or straight at him or her.

Cut
Chop the ball on the off but leave it quite late, so it has almost gone past you, to make it shoot off at a right angle. Very satisfying.

Hook and pull

If the ball lands on the other side of the wicket (leg side) hook it round, or pull it, a bit like you're hitting a baseball.

Now also look online at people doing different things such as:

- Sweep
- Reverse sweep
- Fine edge
- Club
- Morris dancing*

*nothing to do with cricket but it's hilarious and good for your footwork

REMINDER *'Leg side' of the wicket is where the batter's legs are and 'off side' is where their bat is.*

FASCINATING FACTS

The number one male batter in the world at the time of writing is England's Joe Root and he wears the 66 shirt (as in Route 66 – geddit? You know ... the song? Ask your dad.)

The female number one at the time of writing is Australian Alyssa Healy who wears the 77 shirt because it's as close as she could get to wearing the number 7 shirt of David Beckham.

FIELDING

The first thing with fielding is to learn the fielding positions (see page 56).

This is from years of the author of this book looking a bit stupid when given fielding instructions: for example, after being told to go to Silly Mid-Wicket and laughing because you think the captain is making a joke.* Or being told to go to Long Off, running 100 yards in the wrong direction to Fine Leg, then keeping everyone waiting when you have to run back again to the right place.

So, if you know the names of the positions you're never going to look silly ... or, at least not until the ball comes hurtling towards your feet, you panic and run away. It's at this point you realise you should have been working on the Core Skills of Fielding. These are:

- ⚪ Catching
- ⚪ Stopping the ball (if you can't catch it, because it's running along the ground)
- ⚪ Throwing (sometimes from miles away).

Luckily, fielding is one skill you can practise whenever you have a ball handy.

You can practise either with friends, or the dog (if you don't have any friends), or even just against

---

because let's face it, it's a pretty daft name for a position that looks suicidally dangerous.

a wall (if you don't have friends or a dog – or if yours steals balls and eats them like ours).*

Top tips

◯ As much as possible, when catching, cradle the ball with both hands and bring it into your chest. There's much less chance of it popping out of your hands this way.

◯ When you throw a ball, pick a small target, not a big one: for example, aim at one stump, not all three stumps, or 'generally in that direction' – it helps make you more accurate.

That's our dog that steals balls, not our friends – who, as far as I know, aren't really into eating old tennis balls.

Learning to be a Jedi or any kind of meditation is useful for keeping up your concentration when you spend a couple of hours fielding deep with nothing to think about except why that cloud looks like your granny with a machete.

WICKET KEEPING

Practise diving into the swimming pool – left or right – while catching a ball thrown at you. Now strap pads onto your legs, put on a pair of huge gloves and try and do the same (except without the swimming pool, or you'll sink like a stone).

Wicket keeping is a bit like being a goalkeeper in football, except someone (the batter) is standing in front of you, blocking a clear view of where the ball is and you'll be saving fifty or sixty balls every ninety minutes, not four.

The skills needed are in catching, with the reflexes and agility of Spiderman, while wearing more padding than Batman ... and having the concentration of a Grandmaster chess player.

It's a tough gig, but you're right at the centre of things and you'll never get bored.

Top tips
- ◯ Watch the ball
- ◯ No, really watch the ball
- ◯ Position yourself well (closer to the wickets if a spinner is playing, further back for a fast bowler)
- ◯ Make sure you are comfortable crouching
- ◯ As the ball bounces, rise up from the crouch and get ready to catch it if the batter misses.

FASCINATING FACT Former England batsman Alec Stewart, scored 8,463 Test runs. This figure is a bit amazing because Stewart was born on 8 April 1963 (i.e. 8/4/63 – spooky!)

'People talk about cricket being an individual game, but I really don't agree; everything is done in a partnership.'

– Stuart Broad, England cricketer

'He was beautiful and his style was stunning.'

– Singer Katy Perry on former England cricketer, Geoffrey Boycott... I know, weird.

A FUNNY THING HAPPENED...

The New Zealand v England World Cup ODI final in 2019 ranks as the closest final in cricketing history and has been described as the most heart-stoppingly dramatic final ever played.

New Zealand batted first and scored 241 runs. They then bowled very well, leaving England needing 46 runs with just five overs (30 balls) to go and only one top batter left – Ben Stokes. Incredibly, Stokes kept his nerve (and more importantly the strike) and was able to score a very good 31 runs from four overs. However, this left England still needing 15 runs from the last over.

After he had failed to score any runs from the first two balls, it looked unlikely England would win. But then he scored a massive six and the crowd were suddenly on the edge of their seats.

And they would stay that way for the next thirty minutes.

For the next ball, Stokes drove the ball into mid-wicket. Guptill fielded it and chucked the ball back to the striker's end very hard as Stokes was returning to complete a second run. It looked very much like he would be run out and it would all be over but, as Stokes dived for the crease, incredibly, the ball bounced off his bat and raced all the way to boundary behind the wicket.

This gave England six more runs.

But it wasn't quite enough: after thousands of runs scored by dozens of teams, the 2019 World Cup was now tied.

So, they had to play a never-done-before-in-a-world-cup-final Super Over: the country to score the most runs off one over would be crowned world champions.

Once again, it looked like New Zealand had it.

On the final ball of New Zealand's Super Over, after equalling the 15 runs England managed in their over, they just needed two runs to win.

But Martin Guptill was run out by Jos Buttler while attempting to come back for the second run, meaning the Super Over was also tied!

England won on the boundary count-back rule: they had scored 26 boundaries to New Zealand's 17, and won the World Cup.

Unsurprisingly, Ben Stokes was named Man of the Match.

SIR GARFIELD SOBERS

In a chapter that celebrates the arts of bowling, batting and fielding, there probably isn't a better player to shine a spotlight on than the brilliantly named Sir Garfield St Aubrun Sobers (or just plain Sir Garry to his mates).

Born in 1936 in Barbados, he played for the West Indies and is considered one of the greatest cricketers ever (voted by a panel of experts as one of the five Wisden Cricketers of the Century) and almost certainly the greatest all-rounder. Here's why:

- He scored 8,032 test runs (first to score over 8,000)
- He averaged 57.78 runs per innings (in the top five of all time)
- He took 235 test wickets at an average of 34 given away per wicket — both as a seamer and spinner (he really was all-round in everything!

And he took 109 catches...

...putting him in the top few players
of almost any list.

Outside Test cricket Sir Garry scored a huge
28,000 first-class runs and took over 1,000
wickets.

In 1968, playing for Nottinghamshire against
Glamorgan at St Helen's in Swansea, which has a
really short boundary, he was the first player ever
to smash six sixes in one over. His 365 runs
against Pakistan stood as a record total for many
years until it was beaten by fellow countryman
Brian Lara in 2004.

Also, everyone who's met him thinks he's generally
a great guy.

However, just in case you're beginning to think
that's a bit greedy, his ODI cricket career is not
so good: he only played in one match but failed to
score a single run!

CHAPTER 5: FUTURE OF THE GAME

Who plays, where and how

At the start of 2018, the ICC (International Cricket Council) published figures that showed there were over 1.2 billion people playing cricket on planet Earth. That's almost a one-third increase from 2017, which makes cricket the second most popular sport in the world after football.

Some say that if it carries on this way, it might take over from football in the next thirty years.

This is partly helped by the fact that it's the most popular sport in two of the countries with the most people in the world: India and Pakistan. Also cricket is becoming more popular in the USA every year.

But it's mainly due to the fact that cricket is adapting: there are more formats to the game and more people from different backgrounds and with different abilities are being encouraged to play.

So, let's take a closer look at the different ways to play.

VARIATIONS

There are professional and not very professional formats.

International Formats
Test Cricket
One Day Internationals (ODIs)
And Twenty20 (T20s)
See page 50 for details

Other Professional Formats
The Hundred: 100 balls each
Limited Over: 50 overs each (usually)

And here's where it gets really interesting...

Club cricket
Time and/or number of overs decided by the two most important-feeling people from each side (usually the oldest). It's actually the most popular form of cricket.

Declaration cricket
Batting side declares when they think they have a winning number of runs. (Oldest version of cricket there is.)

Indoor cricket
Often six-a-side, useful if you live somewhere where it rains a lot or you're short on space. Surprising it's not more popular in Iceland or the Outer Hebrides.

Kwik cricket
Played by people with short attention spans who evidently can't spell, i.e., small children – especially the sort with a love of anything bright and made of plastic. Great for young beginners.

Garden cricket

Same as street cricket (except it's played in a street), backyard cricket (American garden) or beach cricket (yup, seaside). Often each player plays for themselves (not a team game).

French Cricket

Just not cricket … but still it's surprisingly good fun and there will be a good chance you can persuade your very elderly relatives to play.

Continuous cricket

Hit the ball and run like hell, as the bowler can bowl before you even get back to the crease. Similar games are Bete-ombro in Brazil, and La Placa or La Plaquita in Dominica.

Tape ball cricket

In Pakistan they figured out that if you cover one half of a tennis ball with tape, it will move about in the air like it's being bowled by a professional bowler who has mastered swing. It's hugely fun and very popular – even in Canada (see page 13).

Kilikiti

Also known as Samoan cricket. Loved in New Zealand and Samoa. It came from cricket introduced by British missionaries but they added dance routines and feasting. Also, any number of people can play it and there are no written rules.

Trobriand cricket

Similar to Kilikiti but played in the Trobriand Islands of Papua New Guinea. Also a version of cricket introduced by the British that has been turned into a rave. The home team always wins and players dress up like they're going to war. Brilliant.

Leg cricket

Basically it's like playing cricket when you've forgotten your bat but remembered your legs.

Vigoro

Sort of cricket meets baseball. Mainly played by women.

… and our favourite as kids when stuck in a classroom for hours on sunny days: Pencil Cricket! Can also be played on a calculator but we think the first way is more fun. It's a very easy way to pass the time on trains or anywhere boring (you just need a flat surface to roll a pencil on and a piece of paper) – ask any adult or look up the rules online.

DIVERSITY

With more and more countries getting in on cricket and more people from all walks of life playing for teams around the world, there's now a version of the game to suit most people. For example:

Blind cricket

Invented in Melbourne, Australia, way back in 1922 by two blind factory workers, which must make it one of the oldest disability games going. They used a tin can full of rocks to hear the ball – genius.

The ball is larger and so are the stumps. Also, the ball has bearings inside that make a noise and the stumps are always very bright colours for the partially sighted. Completely blind batters get two goes to hit the ball to make it easier and the bowler has to shout 'Play!' when they release the ball. There have been five World Cups and two T20s.

Others to look out for:

⚪ Wheelchair cricket

⚪ Walking cricket

⚪ Physical disability cricket

FASCINATING FACT Wales has its own international rugby and football teams, but they play with England for cricket, under the control of the England and Wales Cricket Board (ECB). This is why you get English and Welsh players in the 'England' test side. Cardiff Arms Park, which is a famous rugby ground, was originally the main cricket ground in Wales. That honour now belongs to Sophia Gardens, which is also one of several grounds for the only first-class Welsh cricket side, Glamorgan. Not to be confused with the minor counties team, Wales. Clear as a foggy day...

THE ETERNAL SPIRIT OF CRICKET

If cricket was just about throwing, catching or hitting a ball, it wouldn't be nearly as popular as it is today. Like all the best sports, it is just as much about all the stuff around the playing – the things that make it fun and a bit different (very different, really) from any other sport.

It's about learning to bowl a ball like a rocket with pinpoint accuracy, hit it with a bat further than you thought possible, or take a diving catch.

It's about making great friends and doing great things together.

It's about learning that some rules are rules and others have much more to do with what is fair and the right thing to do, which is not in any rule book but is still important.

And let's not forget the things we'll always remember if we play the game long enough: delicious teas – hopefully with cream and cake; the endless skies of sunny days when time slows and the game feels like a dream; the smell of freshly cut grass; gentle clapping; and the sudden call to action when you stride out onto the pitch and anything could happen...

A GREAT CRICKETER YOU'VE NEVER HEARD OF

English cricketer Sydney Barnes (born 1873, died 1967) had possibly the best Test match stats of any bowler ever. He only played in 27 Test matches but took a whopping 189 wickets at 16.43 runs per wicket – incredible!

His first-class career was pretty much the same, with an average of just over 17 runs conceded per wicket, with 719 wickets in just 133 matches.

'The bat is not a toy, it's a weapon.'
– Virat Kohli, 'King'
of Indian cricket

SIR DONALD BRADMAN (AUSTRALIA)

Although one of the early players, Don Bradman (Sir Donald to you) is nearly always in the number one spot when it comes to people's lists of the top ten players of all time.

A quiet man, who didn't seem to enjoy his fame (and he was very famous indeed), Bradman, like a lot of great players, let his bat do the talking.

Amazingly, he only scored six sixes in his entire Test career, which lasted for just over 20 years between 1927 and 1948, with a break for World War Two. However, in that time he scored the most ever runs in one day (300); the most runs in a Test series; the most 200-plus scores in a Test series; the most hundred-plus scores in consecutive matches; and was the fastest player ever to reach (wait for it) 1,000 runs, then 2,000 runs, then 3,000, 4,000, 5,000 and 6,000 Test runs!

In his last game ever, against England in the Ashes in 1948, his batting average stood at over 101 runs. Sadly, although he only needed to score four runs or more to keep it over 100, he was out for a duck (no runs) – finishing on an average of 99.94 – 0.06 short of 100!

Legend has it he was only out for nought because he had tears in his eyes.

However, 99 average or 100, there is no denying he was the most successful batter of all time – 66 per cent better, in fact, than Adam Voges who is placed second in batting averages. It is almost certain that in no other sport has there been a player on the number one spot who is so much better than the second best.

Choosing who to include among all the great players that cricket has graced us with over the last 150 or so years was one of the hardest things I have had to do, while chained to the desk at Stupendous Sports HQ. In the end I had to take twenty of my favourites and pick the selection out of a hat. If I haven't included a player you are sure should be there, please forgive me … then go out and buy lots of copies of Cracking Cricket, so the next version is twice the size and has twice as many spotlights on the greats! Or send your suggestions to us for our website!

In the meantime, you could have fun (and possibly learn a lot of interesting things) by looking up the stories of some of the players below, all greats, who could have been included:

Wasim Akram
Curtly Ambrose
Ian Botham
Sophie Ecclestone
Charlotte Edwards
Jhulan Goswami
Sir Richard Hadlee
Shabnim Ismail
Imran Khan

- Brian Lara
- Muttiah Muralitharan
- Ricky Ponting
- Viv Richards
- Joe Root
- Kumar Sangakkara
- Somjeet Singh
- Dale Steyn

FASCINATING STATS

LAST 10 WORLD CUP CHAMPIONS
(AND RUNNERS UP)

Year	Won by	Score	Runners up
1982	Australia	152/7 (59 overs) won by 3 wickets	England 151/5 (60 overs)
1988	Australia	129/2 (44.5 overs) won by 8 wickets	England 127/7 (60 overs)
1993	England	195/5 (60 overs) won by 67 runs	NZ 128 (55.1 overs)
1997	Australia	165/5 (47.4 overs) won by 5 wickets	NZ 164 (49.3 overs)
2000	NZ	184 (48.4 overs) won by 4 runs	Australia 180 (49.1 overs)
2005	Australia	215/4 (50 overs)	India 117 (46 overs)
2009	England	167/6 (46.1 overs) won by 4 wickets	NZ 166 (47.2 overs)
2013	Australia	259/7 (50 overs) won by 114 runs	West Indies 145 (43.1 overs)
2017	England	228/7 (50 overs) won by 9 runs	India 219 (48.4 overs)
2022	Australia	356/5 (50 overs) won by 71 runs	England 285 (43.4 overs)

UK COUNTY CHAMPIONSHIP WINNERS

Year	Won by	Runners-up
2009	Kent	Sussex
2010	Sussex	Kent
2011	Kent	Sussex
2012	Kent	Essex
2013	Sussex	Yorkshire
2014	Kent	Surrey
2015	Yorkshire	Kent
2016	Kent	Sussex
2017	Lancashire	Yorkshire
2018	Hampshire	Yorkshire
2019	Kent	Yorkshire

GREAT STATS In 1958, Australian cricketer, Betty Wilson became the first player to bag a 10-wicket haul and score over a hundred runs in the same Test match.

ICC WOMEN'S T20 WORLD CUP

Year	Winners	Result	Runners-up
2009	England	86/4 (in 17 overs) won by 6 wickets	NZ 85 (in 20 overs)
2010	Australia	106/8 (in 20 in overs) won by 3 runs	NZ 103/6 (in 20 overs)
2012	Australia	142/4 (in 20 overs) won by 4 runs	England 138/9 (in 20 overs)
2014	Australia	106/4 (in 15 overs) won by 6 wickets	England 105/8 (in 20 overs)
2016	West Indies	149/2 (in 19 overs) won by 8 wickets	Australia 148/5 (in 20 overs)
2018	Australia	106/2 (in 15.1 overs) won by 8 wickets	England 105 (in 19.4 overs)
2020	Australia	184/4 (in 20 overs) won by 85 runs	India 99 (in 19.1 overs)

WOMEN'S ASHES

Series	Years	Result	Tests	Australia	England	Draw
19	2013	England	1	0	0	1
20	2013–14	Australia	1	0	1	0
21	2015	England	1	1	0	0
22	2017–18	Australia	1	0	0	1
23	2019	England	1	0	0	1
24	2021–22	Australia	1	0	0	1

WOMEN'S TEST MATCHES HIGHEST CAREER BATTING AVERAGE

Player	Career	Matches	High Score	Average	100	50	0
D.A. Annetts (AUS-W)	1987–1992	10	193	81.90	2	6	0
E.A. Perry (AUS-W)	2008–2022	10	213	75.20	2	3	0
L. Hill (AUS-W)	1975–1977	7	118	62.37	1	2	0
E. Bakewell (ENG-W)	1968–1979	12	124	59.88	4	7	0
B.J. Haggett (AUS-W)	1987–1992	10	144	58.61	2	4	0
B.R. Wilson (AUS-W)	1948–1958	11	127	57.46	3	3	0
K.L. Rolton (AUS-W)	1995–2009	14	209	55.66	2	5	3
D.A. Hockley (NZ-W)	1979–1996	19	126	52.04	4	7	1
S. Agarwal (IND-W)	1984–1995	13	190	50.45	4	4	1
H. Kala (IND-W)	1999–2006	7	110	50.30	2	3	1

WOMEN'S ODI BOWLING RANKINGS 2022

Player	Career	Wickets
J. Goswami (IND–W)	2002–2022	252
S. Ismail (SA–W)	2007–2022	191
C.L. Fitzpatrick (AUS–W)	1993–2007	180
A. Mohammed (WI–W)	2003–2022	180
K.H. Brunt (ENG–W)	2005–2022	170
E.A. Perry (AUS–W)	2007–2022	161
S.R. Taylor (WI–W)	2008–2022	152
Sana Mir (PAK–W)	2005–2019	151

FUNNY FACTS

There has only ever been one Olympic games where cricket was played. It was in 1900 and only two countries fielded teams: Great Britain and France. Not surprisingly (as the French don't play much cricket – even French cricket [see page 95]), France lost by miles, only managing 23 runs in their second innings. As France invented the modern Olympics, this might be why cricket has not been played again!

LAST 10 WORLD CUP CHAMPIONS
(AND RUNNERS UP)

Year	Won by	Score	Runners up
1983	India	183 all out (55 overs) won by 43 runs	West Indies 140 all out (52 overs)
1987	Australia	253/5 (50 overs) won by 7 runs	England 246/8 (50 overs)
1992	Pakistan	249/6 (50 overs) won by 22 runs	England 227 all out (49.2 overs)
1996	Sri Lanka	245/3 (46.2 overs) won by 7 wickets	Australia 241/7 (50 overs)
1999	Australia	133/2 (20.1 overs) won by 8 wickets	Pakistan 132 all out (39 overs)
2003	Australia	359/2 (50 overs) won by 125 runs	India 234 all out (39.2 overs)
2007	Australia	281/4 (38 overs) won by 53 runs	Sri Lanka 215/8 (36 overs)
2011	India	277/4 (48.2 overs) won by 6 wickets	Sri Lanka 274/6 (50 overs)
2015	Australia	186/3 (33.1 overs) won by 7 wickets	New Zealand 183 all out (45 overs)
2019	England	241 all out (50 overs) Tiebreak: won by 9 fours	New Zealand 241/8 (50 overs)

UK COUNTY CHAMPIONSHIP WINNERS

Year	Won by	Runners-up
2010	Nottinghamshire	Somerset
2011	Lancashire	Warwickshire
2012	Warwickshire	Somerset
2013	Durham	Yorkshire
2014	Yorkshire	Warwickshire
2015	Yorkshire	Middlesex
2016	Middlesex	Somerset
2017	Essex	Lancashire
2018	Surrey	Somerset
2019	Essex	Somerset
2020	*Not held due to COVID-19*	
2021	Warwickshire	Lancashire

T20

The ICC T20 World Cup is held every two years. However, due to the COVID-19 pandemic and some restructuring, there was no T20 World Cup event for five years. However, to put things right, there were two T20 World Cups in two years (2021 and 2022).

Year	Winners	Result	Runners-up
2007	India	5 runs	Pakistan
2009	Pakistan	8 wickets	Sri Lanka
2010	England	7 wickets	Australia
2012	West Indies	36 runs	Sri Lanka
2014	Sri Lanka	6 wickets	India
2016	West Indies	4 wickets	England
2021	Australia	8 wickets	New Zealand
2022	England	5 wickets	Pakistan

GREAT STATS In more modern times, South Africa's A.B. de Villiers holds the record for the fastest ODI century of all time. He took just 31 balls to reach 100 runs against the West Indies in Johannesburg in 2015. He probably had a bus to catch.

ASHES

Year	Won by	Result
2005	England	2-1 (5)
2006/07	Australia	5-0 (5)
2009	England	2-1 (5)
2010/11	England	3-1 (5)
2013	England	3-0 (5)
2013/14	Australia	5-0 (5)
2015	England	3-2 (5)
2017/18	Australia	4-0 (5)
2019	drawn	2-2 (5)
2021/22	Australia	4-0 (5)

INDIAN PREMIER LEAGUE

Year	Winners	Result	Runners-up
2011	Chennai Super Kings	58 runs	Royal Challengers Bangalore
2012	Kolkata Knight Riders	5 wickets	Chennai Super Kings
2013	Mumbai Indians	23 runs	Chennai Super Kings
2014	Kolkata Knight Riders	3 wickets	Kings XI Punjab
2015	Mumbai Indians	41 runs	Chennai Super Kings
2016	Sunrisers Hyderabad	8 runs	Royal Challengers Bangalore
2017	Mumbai Indians	1 run	Rising Pune Supergiant
2018	Chennai Super Kings	8 wickets	Sunrisers Hyderabad
2019	Mumbai Indians	1 run	Chennai Super Kings
2020	Mumbai Indians	5 wickets	Delhi Capitals
2021	Chennai Super Kings	27 runs	Kolkata Knight Riders
2022	Gujarat Titans	7 wickets	Rajasthan Royals

ASIA CUP

Year	Format	Winner	Runners up
1995	ODI	India	Sri Lanka
1997	ODI	Sri Lanka	India
2000	ODI	Pakistan	Sri Lanka
2004	ODI	Sri Lanka	India
2008	ODI	Sri Lanka	India
2010	ODI	India	Sri Lanka
2012	ODI	Pakistan	Bangladesh
2014	ODI	Sri Lanka	Pakistan
2016	T20	India	Bangladesh
2018	ODI	India	Bangladesh

FASCINATING FACT In 2018, minnows Scotland, who are not known for playing top-flight cricket internationally, beat mighty England by six runs, at a One Day International in Edinburgh. It was also Scotland's highest ever ODI score.

TOP 10 TEST RUN SCORERS

Batsman	Runs	Matches	Innings	Average	High Score
Sachin Tendulkar (India)	15,921	200	329	53.79	248
Ricky Ponting (Australia)	13,378	168	287	51.85	257
Jacques Kallis (South Africa)	13,289	166	280	55.37	224
Rahul Dravid (India)	13,288	164	286	52.31	270
Alastair Cook (England)	12,472	161	291	45.35	294
Kumar Sangakkara (Sri Lanka)	12,400	134	233	57.41	319
Brian Lara (West Indies)	11,953	131	232	52.89	400
Shivnarine Chanderpaul (West Indies)	11,867	164	280	51.37	203
Mahela Jayawardene (Sri Lanka)	11,814	149	252	49.85	374
Allan Border (Australia)	11,174	156	265	50.56	205

TOP 10 TEST MATCH BOWLERS

Player	Career	Matches	Inns	Balls	Runs	Wickets
M. Muralitharan (ICC/SL)	1992–2010	133	230	44039	18180	800
S.K. Warne (AUS)	1992–2007	145	273	40705	17995	708
J.M. Anderson (ENG)	2003–2022	175	325	37505	17491	667
A. Kumble (INDIA)	1990–2008	132	236	40850	18355	619
S.C.J. Broad (ENG)	2007–2022	159	293	31982	15720	566
G.D. McGrath (AUS)	1993–2007	124	243	29248	12186	563
C.A. Walsh (WI)	1984–2001	132	242	30019	12688	519
R. Ashwin (INDIA)	2011–2022	86	162	23089	10666	442
D.W. Steyn (SA)	2004–2019	93	171	18608	10077	439
N.M. Lyon (AUS)	2011–2022	110	207	28583	14047	438

TOP 10 TEST MATCH CATCHERS (NOT WICKET KEEPERS)

Player	Career	Matches	Catches
R. Dravid (ICC/INDIA)	1996–2012	164	210
D.P.M.D. Jayawardene (SL)	1997–2014	149	205
J.H. Kallis (ICC/SA)	1995–2013	166	200
R.T. Ponting (AUS)	1995–2012	168	196
M.E. Waugh (AUS)	1991–2002	128	181
A.N. Cook (ENG)	2006–2018	161	175
S.P. Fleming (NZ)	1994–2008	111	171
G.C. Smith (ICC/SA)	2002–2014	117	169
B.C. Lara (ICC/WI)	1990–2006	131	164
J.E. Root (ENG)	2012–2022	124	164

FASCINATING FACT Although there are 31 countries that play cricket on the international stage, only 12 have qualified for Test status. The first countries to acquire this status were England and Australia (1877) and the latest was Afghanistan (2018).

KEYWORDS AND WHAT THEY MEAN

All-rounder

Any player who can bat and bowl well.

Bails

The small pieces of wood that are balanced on top of the stumps. They both make up the wicket.

Ball tampering
Changing the ball by scuffing or cutting into the surface, splitting the seam of the ball, or applying substances other than sweat or spit. Illegal!

Batting average
The number of runs a batsman has scored per innings over his or her career, averaged out.

Beamer
A ball that does not bounce but shoots straight at the batter at head height. Dangerous.

Belter
A pitch that is good for batters and not bowlers.

Bodyline (aka 'leg theory')
A tactic where the bowler aims at the batter rather than the wicket. This is now illegal.

Bosie

An Australian name for a googly. Came from the inventor, B.J.T. Bosanquet.

Bouncer

A short-pitched ball that bounces up at the batter at chest or head height.

Bump ball

A ball that is hit straight into the ground, then caught by a fielder. Looks like a catch but it isn't.

Bunny

A player who frequently gets out to one particular bowler.

Bunsen

A pitch good for slow bowlers. From Cockney rhyming slang 'Bunsen Burner = turner'.

Bye

A ball that the wicket-keeper can't catch that allows the batting team to take a run. If it comes off the batter's leg it's a 'leg bye'.

Carry your bat
An opening batter who manages to stay in, when all his or her teammates are out.

Century
Scoring 100 runs.

Corridor of uncertainty
Describes the fine line just outside the batter's off stump where he or she is unsure whether to leave or play the ball.

Cow corner
Fielding position, thought to have originated at Dulwich College, where there was the corner of a field with – you guessed it – a cow in it.

Crease
The line on the pitch near the wickets. The batter must cross this to score a run.

Dead ball
No runs can be scored nor wickets taken from a dead ball.

Dibbly-dobbly bowlers
Medium-pace bowlers who are good at stopping runs being scored.

Dismiss
To get a batter out.

Dolly
An easy catch.

Doosra
A Hindi and Urdu word which means 'second' (or 'other'). It is the off-spinner's version of the googly.

Duck
Getting out for no runs.

Economy rate
The average number of runs a bowler has scored off the opposition per over.

Extras
Extra runs given to a team for no balls, wides, byes and leg byes.

Four
A shot that gets to the boundary after hitting the ground.

Full toss
Ball that reaches the batter without bouncing; usually not considered good as it's easy to hit.

Gardening
When the batter takes some time out to repair the pitch with his bat.

Good length
The perfect length for a bowler, making the batter play defensively.

Googly
Leg spinning with a twist! Spins into the right-hander or away from the left-hander.

Grubber
A ball that doesn't bounce much, that's very hard to hit (aka shooter).

Innings
A player's, or team's, turn to bat.

Jaffa
A ball that's bowled that the batter can't cope with at all, it's that good.

King pair
Out first ball for zero in both innings. Probably should have gone shopping instead.

LBW (leg before wicket)
Getting out when a ball that will hit the wicket is stopped by a batter's body, usually their legs.

Leg spin
Bowling balls that land ('pitch') on the leg side and spin to the off side.

Lifter
A ball that bounces up unexpectedly.

Lollipop
A really easy ball to smack for six.

Long hop
A ball that lands or pitches short, then bounces up slowly and sort of hangs in the air. Very easy to hit.

Maiden over
The name for an over in which no runs are scored at all.

Manhattan
A bar graph of the runs that are scored during an over. It can look just like the Manhattan skyscrapers skyline. Unless it's a 'maiden over'.

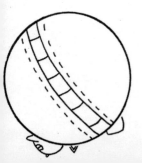

Mankad

When the bowler pretends to bowl but instead, runs out the non-striker by whipping off the bails. The first time a bowler does it is usually just a warning to the batter not to leave his or her crease before the ball is bowled. Good example of fair play.

MCC

The Marylebone Cricket Club, based at Lord's cricket ground in London.

New ball

The bowling team is handed a new ball every eighty overs. More runs and wickets usually happen.

No ball

Illegal delivery bowled by the bowler putting their foot over the crease (line). The batting side gets an extra run. A batter can still hit a no ball, and can only be dismissed by being 'run out'.

Nurdle

When the batter pushes the ball into gaps between the fielders they can be said to be 'nurdling'.

Obstruction

When the batter blocks (or even distracts) a fielder from fielding. This is a no-no.

Occupy the crease

When a batter bats for ages without scoring runs. Quite often ends in a draw.

Off break/spin

An off-spin ball which lands the off side and moves to the leg side, aka 'finger spin'.

Off side

The half of the pitch in front of the batsman as he or she faces the bowler.

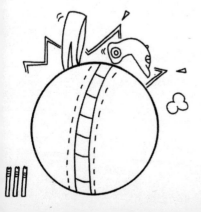

Out

There are ten main ways of getting out: being bowled, being caught, wickets hit by ball or batter, LBW (leg before wicket, as we now know), stumped, timed out, obstruction (including handling the ball), hitting the ball twice and run out. Being injured also counts (retired – in or out, depending) as does being abducted by aliens, carried off by angels, eaten by a lion.

Over

Six balls bowled. Different variations of cricket have a different number of overs. For example, in a one day international, there are 50 overs of play for each team.

Pedantic

Someone who cares too much about rules and definitions and not enough about just enjoying playing and not minding too much if they make a few mistakes. They usually hate it when you say, 'it's only a game.' Or, 'it's really not that important. Chill out!'

Pitch (also 'wicket')
Nice and flat rectangular surface in the centre of the field (22 yards or 20.1 m long) on which bowling and batting happens.

Play on
When a batsman hits the ball but the ball – rather tragically – hits the stumps. Out!

Plumb
When the batsman is clearly LBW. We know it, the umpire knows it, even they do.

Reverse Sweep
Just about the coolest shot you can do – if you get it right: a bit like a scissor kick in football – if you get it wrong people may snigger. Look it up online.

Run-chase
Often in the fourth innings of a first-class or Test match, and both sides agree on a total the batting side needs to get to win. Exciting.

Runner
Sometimes a batter can't run between the wickets (usually through injury), in which case the rules of cricket allow a third player (a bit like a stunt double) to run for him or her.

Single
One run scored by the batter by running once between the wickets.

Six
Shot that goes over the boundary without bouncing.

Sledging
Nothing to do with toboggans, but when players (usually the bowler and batter) trade insults. A bit like a Rap War, but the umpire doesn't beat box.

Slog
Hitting the ball as hard as you can with no style – sometimes works, sometimes doesn't – hugely satisfying, though. Also: tonk, biff, thwack, belt, spank and leather.

Sticky wicket
If it's been raining and the pitch is damp, you can say it's a 'sticky wicket'. Although it's a cricketing expression, it's been pinched by grown-ups to describe any tricky situation in normal life, outside of cricket.

Tail-ender
Players who come in towards the end of an innings, as they are better as bowlers, and are usually a bit rubbish at batting, so they don't last long. Except when they do.

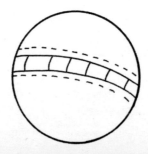

Ton

Another word for a century (100 runs by one batter in one innings).

Twelfth man (or woman)

A substitute fielder (and bringer of drinks/tasty treats) for the team. If called upon to play, he or she is allowed to field wherever they are needed, but they can't bat or bowl.

Walk

When a batter says they're out and walks to the pavilion, even when the umpire hasn't given them out. Again, shows how fair cricket and the best type of cricketers can be.

Adam Gilchrist did this against Sri Lanka in the semi-final of the 2003 World Cup and so did Mike Atherton (sort of), at Trent Bridge in 1998, on 98 not out against South Africa.

Wicket

Hmmm … right … wickets can be used to describe

- ⚪ the 22 yards/20.1 m between the stumps
- ⚪ the stumps together (bails included)
- ⚪ the hitting of these stumps (and getting a batter out – as in 'I got a wicket!')
- ⚪ and – bonkers as it may sound – the act of not being out (e.g. 'Smith and Jones on 180 for the second wicket').

Wide

A ball that pitches (lands) too far away from the batter to hit. The umpire will signal a wide by stretching their arms out horizontally, and an extra run will be added to the total. And the ball will have to be bowled again.

Wisden

Some say the greatest sports book ever produced (after this one, obviously). For the past 158 years, Wisden has been listing all the facts and figures about cricket you can think of and plenty more besides.

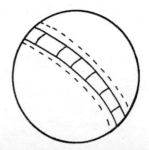

OTHER TITLES IN THE
STUPENDOUS SPORTS SERIES
FANTASTIC FOOTBALL

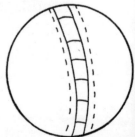

DID YOU KNOW?

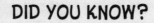 That the earliest form of **football** started in **China** over **2200** years ago. It was called **Cuju** and involved **kicking** the ball into a net without using your **hands**.

In fact there is evidence that football was played in many parts of the world. In **1586** an **English explorer** called **John Davis** came across a tribe of **Inuits** (native people of **Greenland**) playing the game, stopped his ship and joined in.

Modern football **rules** were made up by **English schoolchildren** in the **19th century**.

Football wasn't always that **popular**. It was **banned** in a lot of countries – officially in **Scotland** until **1906**.

Football is easily the most popular sport in the **world**. According to **FIFA**, there are over **250 million players** playing in **200 countries** with over **3.5 billion fans** – nearly half the people in the world!

Foreword and pro tips by Conrad Smith,
ex All Black and double World Cup winner

DID YOU KNOW?

🏉 Rugby started when Webb Ellis picked up a football during a game and ran with it? (He cheated, basically).

🏉 Basketball was created by a rugby coach who wanted an indoor sport to keep his players fit off-season.

🏉 Rugby is played in 119 countries and has over 400 million fans.

WWW.STUPENDOUSSPORTS.COM

THE PLACE FOR KIDS
WHO ARE MAD ON SPORT!

- SPORTS NEWS FOR KIDS
- BOOK AUTHOR VISITS
- CARTOONS
- FUNNY STORIES
- AUDIO DOWNLOADS AND VIDEOS
- NEWS ON FORTHCOMING EVENTS

STUPENDOUS SPORTS FANCLUB!

Look out for special offers on signed books, sports kit, merchandise (toys, stickers, pens – you name it!) and tickets to sporting events!

ACKNOWLEDGMENTS

No book is ever 100 per cent down to one person – as with all the best things in life (including cricket) it's a team effort. I wouldn't have been able to give you a book about cricket nearly half as good without the amazing Matt Cherry and his even more amazing illustrations.

I am also incalculably grateful to Charlie Homewood, Penny Thomas and everyone at Firefly Press for correcting my spelling, checking my facts and laughing in all the right places.

And a quick note on those facts: whilst we have taken care to check rules, stats and facts, cricket is a complex game: rules change, facts can be disputed and records are broken all the time. If anything is wrong or has changed since the book was written, the fault is mine. This is a book about the spirit of cricket more than anything and – much like the elegant and enticing game itself – it may have its flaws and faults but its heart is in the right place, I hope.

FLIP BACK THROUGH
THE LAST FEW
SECTIONS TO WATCH
THIS GUY PLAY
CRICKET!